RV CAMPING
COOKBOOK

100+ RECIPES TO MAKE ON THE ROAD

FOX CHAPEL
PUBLISHING

© 2022 by Fox Chapel Publishing Company, Inc.,
903 Square Street, Mount Joy, PA 17552.

Recipe selection, design, and book design
© Fox Chapel Publishing.
Recipes and photographs © G&R Publishing DBA CQ Products.
Introduction by Mindy Eckart.

ISBN 978-1-4971-0294-1

Library of Congress Control Number: 2021945322

To learn more about the other great books from Fox Chapel
Publishing, or to find a retailer near you, call toll-free
800-457-9112 or visit us at *www.FoxChapelPublishing.com*.

We are always looking for talented authors.
To submit an idea, please send a brief inquiry to
acquisitions@foxchapelpublishing.com.

Printed in China
First printing

CONTENTS

RECIPES

CHAPTER 1: BREAKFAST

AVOCADO BREAKFAST BOATS

PIE IRON OMELET

CHEESY SOUTHERN GRITS

STRAWBERRY FRENCHIES

CHAPTER 2: SIDES

MAPLE ORANGE SQUASH

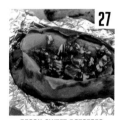

PECAN SWEET POTATOES

LOADED POTATO SALAD

SUMMER SALAD

CHOPPED SALAD WITH JALAPEÑO DRESSING

PEPPERONI PASTA SALAD

CHAPTER 3: MAINS

ALFREDO BACON PIZZA

ONE-POT LASAGNA

BBQ PORK BURGERS

SWEET POTATO CHILI

STUFFED PORTOBELLOS

CHAPTER 4:
APPS, TREATS, AND EXTRAS

BACON CORN DIP

SKILLET OREO ROLLS

BERRY ANGEL CAKES

BACON S'MORES

CINNAMON SENSATION S'MORES

TROPICAL S'MORES

INTRODUCTION

Greetings, fellow RV campers! It's time to hit the open road and allow your RV to take you amazing places. Meals while camping add so many enjoyable memories to RV trips. Whether you're creating the meal or eating it with family and friends by the campfire, food is part of the adventure.

RV Camping Cookbook features delicious, simple-to-prepare fare perfect for on-the-road dining. If you're looking for a quick and easy dinner, a large family brunch, or an around-the-campfire lunch, these recipes have it covered.

Before you go, it's important to spend some time planning. The importance of menu planning before you go cannot be overstated. Not only does it deliver great food, it also ensures your RV is equipped with everything you need.

Having basic kitchen tools and cookware is a must. At minimum, you should have the cooking utensils and tools on the Essential Kitchen Tools checklist and be sure that any bakewear *fits your RV oven*. Use the tools on the list of Essential Campfire Tools to make campfire cooking safe and easy. If you're planning to grill, remember to check your propane or charcoal supply prior to your camping trip, and make sure to keep a supply of dry wood, kindling wood, newspaper, and fire starters to make building the perfect cooking fire a snap.

A well-stocked pantry and refrigerator can make all the difference when RV camping. Use the Essential Pantry and Refrigerator Items checklist to make sure you remember all the standard spices and ingredients you'll need on the road. Don't forget non-food essential items like paper goods, heavy-duty foil and foil pans, and tableware. (A first-aid kit should also be stored in your RV's kitchen or bathroom.) Create your menu based around your travel plans. If you'll be fishing, digging for clams, or visiting local markets, choose meals that will use the ingredients you'll catch or find there.

Above all, assign every item a designated space in your RV. Doing so helps in the critical goal of optimizing space, and in locating what you need when you need it.

Now, it is time to load up the RV, grab your family and friends and don't forget your *RV Camping Cookbook*! The great outdoors is calling your name and your cooking adventures await!

ESSENTIAL PANTRY AND REFRIGERATOR ITEMS

- ☐ eggs
- ☐ butter
- ☐ milk
- ☐ standard spices: salt, pepper, garlic powder, basil, red pepper flakes, and a hearty steak seasoning
- ☐ hamburgers
- ☐ hot dogs
- ☐ hamburger and hot dog rolls
- ☐ breads of choice
- ☐ sugar
- ☐ flour
- ☐ coffee and tea
- ☐ biscuit mix
- ☐ nonstick cooking spray
- ☐ olive oil
- ☐ graham crackers, chocolate bars, and marshmallows for s'mores
- ☐ paper goods (paper towels, napkins)
- ☐ heavy-duty foil and foil pans
- ☐ dish cloths and towels
- ☐ tableware—silverware, plates, bowls, and cups
- ☐ a first-aid kit

ESSENTIAL KITCHEN TOOLS

- ☐ stackable pots and pans
- ☐ nested mixing bowls
- ☐ silicone muffin cups
- ☐ a baking sheet
- ☐ an oven-safe baking dish
- ☐ a coffee pot
- ☐ an electric fry pan
- ☐ a slow cooker or pressure cooker
- ☐ a spatula
- ☐ slotted spoons
- ☐ whisks
- ☐ sharp knives
- ☐ measuring cups and spoons
- ☐ a can opener
- ☐ a bottle opener
- ☐ a pair of scissors

ESSENTIAL CAMPFIRE TOOLS

- ☐ a cast iron pan
- ☐ a Dutch oven
- ☐ skewers
- ☐ a pie iron
- ☐ an over-the-fire grate
- ☐ long, metal tongs
- ☐ a long, metal spatula
- ☐ a long, metal meat fork
- ☐ a long lighter
- ☐ a digital meat thermometer
- ☐ propane or charcoal
- ☐ dry wood, kindling wood, newspaper, and fire starters

CHAPTER 1: BREAKFAST

PINEAPPLE BREAD
Makes one 5" x 9" loaf OVEN

INGREDIENTS
- 1 C. sugar
- ½ C. vegetable oil
- ¾ C. pineapple juice
- 8 oz. can crushed pineapple in juice
- 1 T. baking powder
- 3 C. flour
- ¾ C. chopped macadamia nuts

Preheat oven to 350°F. Lightly grease a 5" x 9" loaf pan and line with wax paper. In a large bowl, combine eggs, vegetable oil, pineapple juice, crushed pineapple including pineapple juice from can, and sugar. Mix well. Into a separate bowl, sift baking powder and flour. Stir flour mixture into pineapple mixture until well combined. Fold in chopped macadamia nuts.

Pour batter into prepared pan. Bake in oven for 50 to 60 minutes or until a toothpick inserted in center of loaf comes out clean.

AVOCADO BREAKFAST BOATS
Makes 4 servings CAMPFIRE

INGREDIENTS
- 2 avocados
- 4 eggs
- 4 T. bacon bits
- Monterey Jack cheese, shredded
- Salt and pepper

Halve avocados and remove pits. Scoop out a little of each center to make room for an egg; mash and reserve. Set each half upright in a nest of foil placed on a larger piece of foil. Crack an egg into each avocado half and sprinkle with 1 tablespoon each bacon bits and shredded Monterey Jack cheese; season with salt and pepper. Seal outer foil around nests and set on coals for 15 minutes, rotating several times but keeping upright. Spoon reserved mashed avocado on top and serve.

BACON CHEDDAR MUFFINS

Makes 6 muffins OVEN

INGREDIENTS
- 1 C. flour
- 2½ tsp. sugar
- 1 tsp. baking powder
- ⅛ tsp. salt
- ¾ tsp. garlic powder
- 1 green onion, chopped
- 2½ T. Parmesan cheese, grated
- ½ C. Cheddar cheese, shredded
- 3 strips bacon, cooked and crumbled
- 1 egg, beaten
- ¼ C. milk
- ¼ C. vegetable oil

Preheat oven to 400˚F. Lightly grease six muffin cups and set aside.

In a large bowl, combine flour, sugar, baking powder, salt, garlic powder, chopped green onion, grated Parmesan cheese, shredded Cheddar cheese, and crumbled bacon. In a separate bowl, using a whisk, combine egg, milk, and vegetable oil. Mix well and stir mixture into dry ingredients, mixing just until moistened.

Spoon batter into prepared muffin cups. Bake in oven for 20 minutes or until a toothpick inserted in center of muffins comes out clean.

ALMOND FRENCH TOAST

Makes 4 servings STOVETOP

INGREDIENTS
- 1 C. slivered almonds
- 3 eggs
- 1 C. milk
- 3 T. flour
- ¼ tsp. salt
- ½ tsp. baking powder
- ½ tsp. almond extract
- 1 tsp. vanilla
- 8 slices thick-cut bread
- 3 T. vegetable oil
- 3 T. butter
- Powdered sugar for dusting

In a small saucepan over low heat, place slivered almonds. Toast almonds until lightly browned, about 5 to 10 minutes, tossing frequently. Set aside 1½ cups of the toasted slivered almonds.

In a large bowl, using a whisk, combine eggs, milk, flour, salt, baking powder, almond extract, and vanilla. Mix well and soak each slice of bread in milk mixture until saturated. Place soaked slices of bread in a shallow pan and chill in refrigerator at least 30 minutes. Meanwhile, in a large skillet over medium heat, heat vegetable oil and butter. Place toasted slivered almonds in a shallow dish. Press slices of bread, one at a time, in the toasted almonds, until coated. Fry coated bread slices in skillet until golden brown on each side. Remove French toast to a plate and dust with powdered sugar.

BERRY-LICIOUS FRENCH TOAST
Makes 6 to 8 servings `OVEN`

INGREDIENTS

- 1 loaf (1 lb.) sliced cinnamon-raisin bread
- 6 eggs
- 1 tsp. vanilla
- ⅓ C. milk
- ¾ C. heavy cream, divided
- 2 T. pure maple syrup, plus more for serving
- 1 to 1½ C. fresh blueberries and/or raspberries
- 1 C. powdered sugar

Heat oven to 375°F. Lay two big sheets of heavy-duty foil on top of each other on a rimmed baking sheet and spritz with cooking spray. Set the loaf of bread in the center of the foil; fold the edges up around the bottom half of the loaf to hold the bread in place and keep the egg mixture contained. Fan out the bread slices slightly.

In a bowl, beat the eggs. Whisk in the vanilla, milk, ½ cup of the cream, and 2 tablespoons of the maple syrup. Pour the mixture slowly over the top of the bread, making sure to soak both sides of each slice. Scatter the berries over the top, pushing some between the slices. Cover the bread with another big sheet of foil; crimp the edges to seal the bread inside. Bake for 30 to 45 minutes until the eggs are set, removing the top foil during the last 10 minutes if necessary to prevent overbrowning.

Mix the powdered sugar with enough of the remaining cream to make a drizzling consistency. Open the foil and drizzle the glaze over the bread. Serve with maple syrup.

OVERNIGHT APPLE PIE OATMEAL

Makes 4 servings   ⬤ SLOW COOKER

INGREDIENTS

- 1 T. coconut oil, plus more for coating slow cooker
- 2 Gala apples
- 1½ C. coconut milk, plus more, if desired, for serving
- 1½ C. water
- 1 C. steel-cut oats
- ¼ to ½ tsp. sea salt
- 1 tsp. vanilla
- Brown sugar, cinnamon, half-and-half, honey, and/or maple syrup for serving
- Chopped walnuts for serving
- Flaked or toasted coconut for serving

Coat a big slow cooker heavily with coconut oil. Core and dice apples and toss them into the cooker. Add coconut milk, water, steel-cut oats, coconut oil, sea salt, and vanilla. Stir to blend.

Cook on low for 5 to 7 hours, until the apples and oats are tender. Top servings with brown sugar, cinnamon, half-and-half or coconut milk, honey, and/or maple syrup, and a sprinkling of chopped walnuts and/or flaked or toasted coconut.

HONEY BRAN MUFFINS
Makes 12 jumbo muffins `OVEN`

INGREDIENTS
- 2 C. pineapple juice
- 2 C. golden raisins
- 2 C. flour
- 2 tsp. baking soda
- 1 tsp. salt
- 1 C. whole bran cereal
- 1 C. brown sugar
- ½ C. vegetable oil
- ½ C. honey
- Eggs, beaten

In a small bowl, combine pineapple juice and golden raisins. Mix lightly and set aside. In a medium bowl, combine flour, baking soda, and salt. Mix well and stir in whole bran cereal and set aside. In a large bowl, combine brown sugar, vegetable oil, honey, and beaten eggs. Mix well and stir in bran cereal mixture. Stir until well combined and fold in pineapple juice and raisins. Mix well. The batter will be thin. Cover and chill batter in refrigerator overnight.

In morning, preheat oven to 400°F. Lightly grease 12 jumbo muffin cups and stir the chilled batter. Fill each muffin cup ¾ full with batter. Bake in oven for 20 to 25 minutes or until a toothpick inserted in center of muffins comes out clean. Remove muffins from oven and let cool on a wire rack for 10 minutes before removing from cups.

FLUFFY FLAPJACKS
Makes 12 flapjacks `CAMPFIRE`

INGREDIENTS
- 5 eggs
- 2 C. pancake mix
- 2 T. sugar
- ½ tsp. cinnamon
- 2 T. butter, melted
- ½ C. ginger ale

In a bowl, whisk the eggs until well beaten. Add the pancake mix, sugar, and cinnamon. Pour in the butter and ginger ale. Stir until just combined (the mixture will be lumpy).

Heat a griddle or skillet and spritz with cooking spray. Pour the batter onto the hot pan using about ⅓ cup for each pancake. Cook until golden brown on both sides, flipping once.

Serve with butter and maple syrup.

PIE IRON OMELET
Makes 4 omelets `CAMPFIRE`

INGREDIENTS
- 1 C. ham, diced
- ½ C. bell peppers, diced
- ½ C. yellow onion, diced
- 5 eggs
- 2 T. water
- Butter for greasing skillet and pie iron
- 8 oz. tube refrigerated crescent dough sheet
- 8 T. Cheddar cheese, shredded

Toss ham into a bowl. Add bell peppers and onion. In another bowl, scramble eggs with water; cook in a buttered skillet over medium heat until fluffy. Unroll crescent dough sheet and cut into eight equal pieces. Press one piece into a greased pie iron and add ¼ each of the egg and ham mixture and 2 tablespoons shredded Cheddar cheese. Cover with another dough piece and close pie iron. Cook in hot coals until golden brown on both sides. Repeat to make three more.

WALNUT WHOLE WHEAT MUFFINS
Makes 12 muffins `OVEN`

INGREDIENTS
- 1 C. flour
- 1 C. whole wheat flour
- ½ C. sugar
- 1 tsp. baking soda
- 2 tsp. baking powder
- 1 tsp. salt
- ½ tsp. nutmeg
- 6 oz. plain yogurt
- 1 C. milk
- 1 tsp. vanilla
- ½ C. chopped walnuts

Preheat oven to 375°F. Lightly grease 12 muffin cups and set aside. In a large bowl, combine flour, whole wheat flour, sugar, baking soda, baking powder, salt, and nutmeg. In a medium bowl, combine plain yogurt, milk, and vanilla; mix well. Pour yogurt mixture over flour mixture and stir just until blended. Fold in chopped walnuts and mix lightly. Spoon batter into prepared muffins cups. Bake in oven for 18 to 20 minutes or until a toothpick inserted in center of muffins comes out clean. Remove muffins from oven and let cool slightly on a wire rack.

BACON & CHEDDAR PULL-APARTS
Makes 10–14 servings CAMPFIRE

INGREDIENTS
- Two 16.3-oz. tubes flaky layers refrigerated biscuits (we used Pillsbury Grands! Honey Butter flavor)
- ⅔ C. chive and onion cream cheese spread
- ¾ lb. bacon, cooked and crumbled
- 4 green onions, finely chopped
- 8 deli slices Cheddar cheese, quartered

Grease a 9" x 9" aluminum baking pan and set inside a second one. Separate each biscuit into two layers. Spread about 1 teaspoon cream cheese on each piece and top with 1 to 2 teaspoons bacon, ½ teaspoon green onion, and ¼ slice cheese. Make four stacks of eight layers. Set one stack on its side along the side of pan, starting in one corner (side without filling should touch the edge of pan.) Set a second stack in pan at right angles to first stack. Set remaining two stacks around edges to fill pan.

Set pan on risers in a large Dutch oven (we used three canning jar rings). Cover with lid and place on a ring of 12 hot coals with a few more coals on lid. Bake 50 to 60 minutes or until puffy, browned, and no longer doughy. Rotate pot and lid every 15 minutes and check doneness several times, replenishing or removing coals as needed for even baking. (If you prefer, bake the pan in a 350°F oven about 1 hour or until done.)

BACON & AVOCADO OMELET

Makes 4 to 6 servings CAMPFIRE

INGREDIENTS

- 8 slices bacon
- 8 eggs
- 6 T. water
- Salt and pepper to taste
- 3 T. butter
- 1 large avocado, peeled and cut into ½" pieces
- 1½ C. Monterey Jack cheese, shredded
- 2½ C. medium heat salsa

In a medium cast iron skillet over medium-high heat, cook bacon until browned and remove to paper towels to drain. Crumble the bacon and set aside. Drain skillet of fat. In a medium bowl, whisk together eggs, water, salt, and pepper. In the same skillet over medium-high heat, place ¼ of the butter. When butter has melted, swirl skillet until coated. Pour ¼ of the egg mixture into skillet. Heat for about 2 minutes, until egg mixture begins to set at the bottom of the pan. Gently lift edges of egg and push inward so the uncooked part of the egg mixture flows toward the edges. Continue to cook until the center of the omelet starts to look dry, about 2 to 3 minutes. Sprinkle some of the crumbled bacon, avocado pieces, and shredded Monterey Jack cheese over half of the omelet. Cook for 1 minute, until cheese begins to melt. Fold omelet over the filling and slide onto a plate.

   Repeat with remaining egg mixture, bacon, avocado, and shredded cheese to make three more omelets. Serve omelets with salsa.

CHEESY SOUTHERN GRITS

Makes 4 servings CAMPFIRE

INGREDIENTS

- 4 eggs
- 2 T. water
- ¼ lb. bacon
- 2 oz. instant grits
- Butter, salt, and pepper to taste
- Cheddar Jack cheese, shredded

Whisk eggs with water in a small bowl. Cook bacon in a cast iron skillet until crisp; drain bacon strips and crumble, reserving grease in skillet.

   Cook the eggs in the bacon grease, stirring often, until fluffy and done. In each of four serving bowls, mix instant grits with boiling water as directed on package. Stir in butter, salt, and pepper to taste. Top each serving of grits with some scrambled eggs, 2 to 3 tablespoons shredded Cheddar Jack cheese, and crumbled bacon.

MAKE-AHEAD PANCAKE MIX

Makes about 2 servings   MAKE-AHEAD

INGREDIENTS
- 1⅓ C. flour
- 2 tsp. baking powder
- ¼ tsp. salt
- 1½ T. vegetable oil

In a bowl, whisk together flour, baking powder, and salt. Add vegetable oil and mix it in with your hands. Make it before your trip and store in an airtight container at room temperature for several weeks.

BREAKFAST TARTS

Makes 4 servings   OVEN

INGREDIENTS
- 9 to 11 oz. piecrust mix
- 8 slices bacon
- ½ C. Cheddar cheese, shredded
- 3 eggs
- 3 T. milk
- ¼ tsp. nutmeg
- ¼ tsp. pepper

Preheat oven to 425˚F. Prepare pastry for a one-crust pie according to package directions. Divide pastry into four equal parts and roll each part into a 6" circle. Place each pastry circle in a large muffin cup or 6-ounce pastry cup, making pleats so the pastry covers the bottoms and sides of each cup. Poke the surface of each crust with a fork and bake in oven for 8 to 10 minutes, until crusts are lightly browned. Remove crusts from oven and reduce oven temperature to 350˚F.

Meanwhile, in a medium skillet over medium-high heat, cook bacon until crisp. Remove bacon from skillet and drain on paper towels. Crumble two slices bacon into the bottom of each crust and sprinkle with 2 tablespoons of the shredded Cheddar cheese. In a small bowl, combine eggs, milk, nutmeg, and pepper; whisk together well. Pour a portion of the egg mixture over bacon and cheese in each crust. Return to oven for an additional 15 to 20 minutes until eggs are cooked.

MAPLE TWISTS

Makes 16 rolls OVEN

INGREDIENTS

- 4 oz. cream cheese, softened
- ¼ C. powdered sugar
- 2 T. butter, softened
- 1 C. brown sugar
- ½ C. chopped walnuts
- ⅓ C. maple syrup
- 2 C. all-purpose baking mix (we used Bisquick)
- ¼ C. milk
- 2 T. sugar
- 1 egg

Preheat oven to 425°F. In a medium bowl, combine cream cheese, powdered sugar, and butter. Mix well and set aside. In a 9" x 13" baking dish, combine brown sugar, chopped walnuts, and maple syrup. Mix well and spread evenly over bottom of baking dish. In a separate medium bowl, combine baking mix, milk, sugar, and egg until a dough forms. Beat dough vigorously until mixture is smooth. Form dough into a ball and knead eight times on a lightly floured flat surface. Roll the dough into a 9" x 16" rectangle. Spread cream cheese mixture over dough and carefully fold the dough lengthwise into thirds. Press edges of dough to seal. Cut dough into sixteen 1" strips. Gently twist each strip and place twisted strips in baking dish over brown sugar mixture. Bake in oven for 15 minutes. To serve, invert strips onto a serving plate.

STRAWBERRY FRENCHIES

Makes 4 servings CAMPFIRE

INGREDIENTS

- 3 eggs
- ¼ C. milk
- 1 tsp. cinnamon sugar
- Strawberry preserves
- 1 C. sliced strawberries

Whisk together eggs, milk, and cinnamon sugar. Dip one side of a bread slice into egg mixture and set in a greased pie iron, egg side down. Spread with strawberry preserves; arrange ¼ cup sliced strawberries over preserves. Dip another bread slice in egg and place it on top, egg side up. Close iron and cook in hot embers until toasted on both sides. Repeat to make three more. Serve with maple syrup.

RISE & SHINE KEBABS

Makes 4 skewers CAMPFIRE

INGREDIENTS
- 2 nectarines
- 3 red potatoes
- 1 green bell pepper
- 1 red or orange bell pepper
- 12 breakfast sausage links
- Pineapple chunks
- Apple jelly

Pit nectarines and slice into wedges. Cut red potatoes into thin wedges and cut half of each bell pepper into 1" pieces. Slice sausage links in half. Alternately thread pieces of pineapple, nectarine, potato, bell pepper, and sausage onto four skewers. Cook skewers on an oiled grate over medium-low heat about 15 minutes, turning often and brushing with apple jelly, until sausage is done, potatoes are tender, and fruit is lightly browned.

BACON QUICHE TARTS

Makes 10 tarts OVEN

INGREDIENTS
- 12 slices bacon
- 8 oz. cream cheese, softened
- 2 T. milk
- 2 eggs
- ½ C. Swiss cheese, shredded
- 4 green onions, chopped
- 10 oz. can refrigerated flaky biscuit dough

Preheat oven to 375°F. Lightly grease 10 muffin cups and set aside. In a large skillet over medium-high heat, cook bacon until browned. Remove bacon to paper towels to drain. In a medium bowl, combine the cream cheese, milk, and eggs. Using a hand mixer, beat ingredients together until smooth. Fold in shredded Swiss cheese and chopped green onions; set aside.

Separate biscuit dough into 10 biscuits. Press one biscuit into the bottom and up sides of each muffin cup. Crumble bacon and sprinkle half into the bottoms of the filled muffin cups, then spoon 2 tablespoons of the cream cheese mixture into each muffin cup. Bake in oven for 20 to 25 minutes until filling is set and crust is golden brown. Sprinkle the remaining crumbled bacon over each muffin cup and press lightly into the filling. Remove tarts from muffin cups and serve warm.

DEEP DISH BREAKFAST PIZZA
Makes 1 large pizza   CAMPFIRE

INGREDIENTS

- ¾ lb. bacon strips
- ½ red onion, diced
- ½ lb. ground Italian sausage
- 1 lb. frozen pizza dough, thawed
- 1 C. each Cheddar and mozzarella cheese, shredded
- 4 eggs
- 2 T. water
- Garlic powder, salt, and black pepper to taste
- Parmesan cheese, grated

Cook bacon in the pot of a 10" Dutch oven over medium-high heat until crisp; drain on paper towels and pour off grease. Crumble bacon and put in a big bowl. Cook onion and sausage in the pot until meat is browned and crumbly.

Remove from heat and add meat mixture to bowl with bacon; set aside. Let the pot cool, then wipe out excess grease. Line pot with foil and grease lightly. Press dough over the bottom of pot and 1" up the side. Cover with lid and set on a ring of seven hot coals. Partially bake crust for 5 to 8 minutes.

Press meat mixture into partially baked crust; sprinkle with shredded cheeses. In a bowl, whisk together eggs, water, and seasonings; pour evenly over ingredients in crust, letting it seep in without overflowing. Sprinkle with Parmesan cheese. Cover and set on a ring of seven hot coals with 12 more coals scattered on lid. Bake 20 to 25 minutes or until crust is golden brown and eggs are puffed and set. Rotate pot and lid several times and move coals as needed for even baking. Let stand 5 minutes, then lift foil to remove pizza.

CHAPTER 2: SIDES

BALSAMIC VEGGIE SALAD

Makes 4 to 5 servings **STOVETOP**

INGREDIENTS

- 1½ lbs. red potatoes, cubed
- Salt
- ¾ lb. fresh green beans, trimmed and quartered
- ¼ C. chopped fresh basil
- 1 small red onion, chopped
- 1 tomato, diced
- 2.25 oz. can sliced black olives, drained
- Black pepper to taste
- ¾ to 1 C. balsamic vinaigrette

Put the potatoes and 1 tablespoon salt into a big saucepan and add cold water to cover by 2". Cover and bring to a boil. Cook about 10 minutes or until the potatoes are just tender; transfer the potatoes to a big bowl to cool. Dump the beans into the cooking water and boil for 3 to 5 minutes; drain and plunge the beans into ice water.

When everything is cool, add the beans, basil, onion, tomato, and olives to the potatoes. Pour about half the vinaigrette over the salad and stir gently to coat; stir in as much of the remaining vinaigrette as you'd like. Season with salt and black pepper. Chill several hours before serving.

CAMPFIRE PARMESAN CORN

Makes desired number of ears of corn CAMPFIRE

INGREDIENTS
- Butter, softened
- Sweet corn, husked and silk removed
- Parmesan, grated
- Dried rosemary
- Salt and black pepper to taste
- Ice cubes

Spread a generous amount of butter over the entire surface of the sweet corn; sprinkle with grated Parmesan, dried rosemary, salt, and black pepper to taste.

Place the ears on a big piece of foil (up to four ears per piece of foil) and toss on a few ice cubes. Wrap the foil around the corn, leaving a little space inside for air to circulate; seal edges tightly. Place in hot coals for 20 minutes or until the corn is tender, turning the pack occasionally. Remove the pack from the fire using tongs and open carefully.

MAPLE ORANGE SQUASH

Makes 4 servings   GRILL

INGREDIENTS
- 1 lb. butternut squash
- 3 T. olive oil
- ½ C. pure maple syrup
- 1 T. orange zest
- ½ tsp. cinnamon
- Cooking spray
- 3 T. butter, sliced

Preheat your grill to medium heat. Meanwhile peel, seed, and cut butternut squash into 1" cubes and microwave for 2 minutes (or par-cook until barely tender); stir in olive oil. Add pure maple syrup, orange zest, and cinnamon; stir to coat. Spritz a big piece of heavy-duty foil with cooking spray and dump the squash mixture onto the foil; top with butter. Wrap the foil around the squash, leaving a little space inside for air to circulate; seal edges tightly.

    Set the foil pack on the grill, close the lid, and cook for 20 minutes until tender. Open packet carefully and stir before serving.

CHEESY HASH BROWNS

Makes 4 servings   STOVETOP

INGREDIENTS
- 1 small onion
- 2 slices bacon
- 2 T. butter
- 4 large potatoes, peeled and shredded
- 2 eggs
- Salt and pepper to taste
- ½ C. Cheddar cheese, shredded

Chop onion into small pieces. In a large skillet over medium-high heat, cook bacon until browned and remove to paper towels to drain, leaving bacon grease in pan. Crumble bacon and set aside. Return skillet to medium heat and stir butter into bacon drippings. Add chopped onions and shredded potatoes. Cover pan and cook, stirring frequently, until potatoes are golden brown. Crack eggs over potatoes and stir until combined. Sprinkle with salt, pepper, and shredded Cheddar cheese. Continue to cook until eggs are set and cheese is melted

CUCUMBER ASPARAGUS SALAD

Makes 4 to 6 servings **STOVETOP**

INGREDIENTS

- 1¾ C. water
- 1 C. long-grain white rice
- 1½ lbs. asparagus, par-cooked and cooled
- 1 large cucumber, peeled, seeded, and chopped
- 3 green onions, chopped
- 2 T. Dijon mustard
- 1 T. sugar
- 1 T. white wine vinegar
- ½ tsp. dry mustard
- 2½ T. vegetable oil
- 1 tsp. dried dillweed
- 4 small heads butter lettuce

In a medium saucepan over medium heat, bring water to a boil. Add rice, return to a boil, reduce heat, cover, and let cook until water is absorbed and rice is tender, about 20 minutes. Fluff rice with a fork, remove from heat, and let cool to room temperature.

Cut par-cooked asparagus into 1" pieces. Add asparagus pieces, chopped cucumber, and chopped green onions to rice. In a medium bowl, whisk together Dijon mustard, sugar, white wine vinegar, dry mustard, vegetable oil, and dried dillweed. Pour dressing over rice ingredients and toss until well incorporated. Fill a large serving bowl with torn lettuce and top with rice and asparagus mixture.

PECAN SWEET POTATOES

Makes 4 servings **CAMPFIRE**

INGREDIENTS

- 4 sweet potatoes
- ⅓ C. butter, melted
- ½ C. brown sugar
- ½ C. chopped pecans

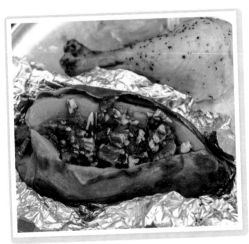

Pierce sweet potatoes and wrap in foil. Bake in hot coals 45 to 60 minutes until tender, turning twice. Mix butter, brown sugar, and pecans. Cut potatoes open and top with pecan mixture.

SPINACH ARTICHOKE MELTS
Makes 3 servings `STOVETOP`

INGREDIENTS

- Butter, softened
- ½ tsp. minced garlic
- 1 T. flour
- ½ C. milk
- 1½ T. cream cheese spread
- ½ C. mozzarella cheese, shredded
- ½ C. Parmesan cheese, grated
- ½ tsp. red pepper flakes
- ½ tsp. black pepper
- ½ C. sour cream
- 6.7 oz. jar artichokes, drained and chopped
- ½ C. grilled chicken breast, diced
- ½ C. frozen chopped spinach, thawed, drained, and squeezed dry
- 6 slices sourdough bread

Melt 1 tablespoon butter in a medium saucepan over medium heat. Add the garlic and cook for 1 minute. Whisk in the flour to make a paste, then cook another minute or so. Slowly add the milk, cooking and stirring for a minute or two, until slightly thickened. Add the cream cheese spread, the mozzarella and Parmesan cheeses, red pepper flakes, and black pepper; stir until the cheese melts. Stir in the sour cream until smooth. Finally, stir in the artichokes, chicken, and spinach; remove from the heat.

Heat a large skillet or griddle over medium-low heat. Meanwhile, spread a few tablespoons of the artichoke mixture over half the bread slices and top with the remaining bread slices; butter the outside of each slice and lay the sandwiches in the hot pan. Cook until both sides are golden brown and the filling is hot, turning halfway through cooking.

CORNBREAD MINIS WITH CHIPOTLE BUTTER

Makes 8 servings `CAMPFIRE`

INGREDIENTS

- 8.5 oz. corn muffin mix
- Eggs and milk as indicated on muffin mix package
- ¼ C. Pepper Jack cheese, shredded
- 2 T. chopped canned chilis, drained
- ¼ C. whole kernel corn, drained
- 2 chipotle peppers in adobo, chopped
- ¼ C. butter, softened
- 2 T. honey

Stir together corn muffin mix and the eggs and milk called for on the muffin mix package. Stir in shredded Pepper Jack cheese, chilis, and whole kernel corn. Grease pie irons, fill with batter, and close; hold level above warm coals until both sides are brown, turning often. Stir together chipotle peppers, butter, and honey to top.

LOADED POTATO SALAD

Makes 8 to 10 servings `STOVETOP`

INGREDIENTS

- 3 lbs. red-skinned potatoes
- Salt
- 3 eggs
- 8 dill pickle spears, diced
- 3 celery ribs, sliced
- ½ medium red onion, chopped
- ⅔ C. mayonnaise
- 2 T. stone-ground mustard
- 2½ T. apple cider vinegar
- 2 T. chopped fresh dill
- Black pepper to taste

In a big saucepan, cook the potatoes in salted boiling water until just tender; drain and let cool.

In the meantime, put the eggs in a single layer in a saucepan and add water to cover by 1". Bring to a boil; cover, remove from the heat, and let stand 15 minutes. Drain off the hot water and fill the saucepan with cold water and ice; let stand until the eggs are cool. Peel under cold running water and set aside.

Cut the cooled potatoes into bite-size pieces and chop the eggs; dump into a big bowl along with the pickles, celery, and onion.

In a small bowl, stir together the mayonnaise, mustard, vinegar, and dill; pour the mixture over the vegetables in the bowl. Season with salt and black pepper and mix gently to blend.

MACARONI CASSEROLE

Makes 4 to 6 servings `STOVETOP`

INGREDIENTS

- 32 oz. uncooked macaroni
- 1½ lbs. ground beef
- 1 onion, chopped
- 1 green bell pepper, chopped
- Two 29 oz. cans tomato sauce

In a large pot of lightly salted water, cook macaroni according to package directions, until al dente. Drain pasta. In a large skillet over medium heat, cook ground beef until cooked throughout. Add chopped onions and sauté until onions are softened. Add chopped green bell pepper and tomato sauce. Continue to cook until heated throughout and green peppers are softened. To serve, place cooked pasta evenly on four to six serving plates. Spoon a generous amount of the ground beef mixture over pasta and serve.

BAKED ALMOND RICE CASSEROLE

Makes 4 to 6 servings `OVEN`

INGREDIENTS

- 8 C. water
- 4 C. uncooked brown rice
- ½ C. butter
- 4 green onions, chopped
- Two 10¾ oz. cans cream of mushroom soup
- 1 C. fresh mushrooms, sliced
- 1 C. toasted slivered almonds
- 1½ C. Cheddar cheese, shredded

Preheat oven to 350°F. In a large saucepan over medium-high heat, bring water to a boil. Add rice, reduce heat, cover, and let simmer for 20 minutes, stirring occasionally.

Meanwhile, in a small saucepan over medium heat, place butter. When butter has melted, stir in chopped green onions and sauté until onions are softened. Stir in cream of mushroom soup, cooked brown rice, mushrooms, and toasted slivered almonds. Spoon half of the mixture into 1½-quart baking dish. Sprinkle half of the shredded Cheddar cheese over the mixture and top with remaining half of the rice mixture. Sprinkle remaining half of the shredded Cheddar cheese over rice mixture and bake in oven for 20 minutes or until casserole is heated throughout and cheese is melted.

GARDEN PASTA SALAD

Makes 4 servings `STOVETOP`

INGREDIENTS

- 2 C. garden rotini pasta
- ½ C. bell pepper (any color), diced
- Cherry tomatoes, sliced
- ¼ C. Kalamata olives, sliced
- Italian dressing

Cook pasta in boiling water to al dente according to package directions; rinse in cold water and drain well. Combine the cooked pasta, bell pepper, cherry tomatoes, and Kalamata olives. Stir in enough Italian dressing to moisten. Chill until serving time.

CALIFORNIA CABBAGE SALAD

Makes 4 to 6 servings STOVETOP

INGREDIENTS

- 3 oz. chicken-flavored ramen noodles
- ¼ C. butter
- ½ C. sesame seeds
- ½ C. slivered almonds
- 1 large head Napa cabbage, shredded
- 6 green onions, chopped
- ¼ C. vegetable oil
- ¼ C. rice wine vinegar
- 1 T. soy sauce
- 1 T. sesame oil
- 2 T. sugar

Crush the ramen noodles. In a medium skillet over medium heat, place butter. When butter has melted, add crushed ramen noodles, sesame seeds, and slivered almonds. Stir until noodles, seeds, and almonds are lightly toasted, stirring frequently to prevent burning. Add seasoning mix from ramen noodles and blend well.

In a large bowl, place shredded cabbage and chopped green onions. Add flavored noodles, sesame seeds, and slivered almonds. In a medium bowl, whisk together vegetable oil, rice wine vinegar, soy sauce, sesame oil, and sugar. Whisk thoroughly, until sugar is dissolved. Pour mixture over salad and toss until evenly coated.

CREAMY COLESLAW

Makes 6 to 8 servings NO-COOK

INGREDIENTS

- 4 to 5 C. cabbage, shredded
- ½ C. red onion, chopped
- ½ C. green pepper, diced
- 2 celery ribs, chopped
- ¾ C. mayonnaise
- 2 T. sugar
- 2 T. apple cider vinegar
- 2 T. olive oil
- 1 tsp. sea salt
- Black pepper to taste

Combine all vegetables in a bowl. In another bowl, whisk mayonnaise, sugar, apple cider vinegar, and olive oil with sea salt and pepper to taste. Toss with cabbage. Chill.

FIRE-ROASTED BRUSSELS SPROUT SKEWERS

Makes 4 servings GRILL

INGREDIENTS
- 1 lb. Brussels sprouts, par-cooked
- 2 generous T. spicy brown mustard
- 2 T. olive oil
- Salt and pepper to taste

Toss trimmed and par-cooked sprouts into bowl with mustard, olive oil, and salt and pepper. Let marinate 30 minutes. To cook, thread sprouts on skewers and grill on oiled grate over medium-hot coals until sprouts are tender (3 to 6 minutes).

ALL-PURPOSE SEASONING MIX

For RV cooking convenience, make this delicious All-Purpose Seasoning Mix ahead of time and store it with your supply of staples. It's incredibly versatile and infuses flavor into all kinds of dishes.

Combine 2 tablespoons each garlic powder and ground cumin, 1 tablespoon each ground coriander, smoked paprika, and sea salt, and 1½ teaspoons black pepper. Sprinkle on pieces of meat or stir into ground meat mixtures while cooking. To make a meat rub, mix 1½ tablespoons seasoning mix with 3 to 4 tablespoons olive oil and rub into chicken, beef, or pork before grilling. Store seasoning in a small, airtight container.

CHOPPED SALAD WITH JALAPEÑO DRESSING

Makes 2 servings **STOVETOP**

INGREDIENTS

- ¼ C. pickled jalapeños, finely chopped
- ¼ C. mayonnaise
- ¼ C. ranch dressing or sour cream
- 2 T. cilantro, chopped
- 1 T. lime juice
- ½ tsp. paprika
- 1 to 2 T. milk or half-and-half
- 15 oz. can yellow hominy, drained, rinsed, and patted dry
- Cayenne pepper to taste
- 4 C. Romaine lettuce, chopped
- Grape tomatoes, halved
- 1 C. rotisserie chicken or leftover cooked chicken
- 1 mango, peeled, seeded, and sliced
- 1 avocado, peeled, seeded, and sliced
- 1 bell pepper (any color), sliced
- Queso fresco or feta cheese, crumbled
- Pumpkin seeds (pepitas)

In a mason jar or other lidded container, combine the pickled jalapeños, mayonnaise, ranch dressing or sour cream, cilantro, lime juice, and paprika. Pour in enough milk to reach the consistency you like. Cover, shake, and chill until serving time.

In a medium skillet, heat hominy over low heat until just beginning to brown, stirring occasionally; sprinkle with cayenne pepper.

On a big tray, arrange the lettuce, hominy, tomatoes, chicken, mango, avocado, and bell pepper. Serve with the chilled dressing, queso fresco or feta, and pumpkin seeds alongside.

GUACAMOLE SALAD

Makes 4 servings **NO-COOK**

INGREDIENTS

- 2 avocados, peeled
- ¼ C. lemon juice
- ½ C. sour cream
- 1 clove garlic, minced
- 2 tsp. fresh dill
- 1 tsp. Worcestershire sauce
- 1 small tomato, chopped

Mash one avocado in medium bowl. Stir in lemon juice, sour cream, minced garlic, fresh dill, Worcestershire sauce, and tomato. Chop remaining avocado into pieces and add to bowl. Cover and chill.

SUMMER SALAD

Makes 4 servings **NO-COOK**

INGREDIENTS

- 2 tomatoes, diced
- 1 cucumber, diced
- 2 avocados, peeled and diced
- ¼ of a red onion, chopped
- 3 to 4 T. lime vinaigrette
- Salt and black pepper to taste
- Crumbled feta cheese

In a serving bowl, combine tomatoes, cucumber, avocados, and red onion. Drizzle with 3 to 4 tablespoons lime vinaigrette and stir gently to coat. Season with salt and black pepper and stir again. Before serving, top with a little crumbled feta cheese.

PEPPERONI PASTA SALAD
Makes 6 to 8 servings STOVETOP

INGREDIENTS
- 6 oz. small shell pasta
- 1 C. pepperoni, chopped
- 4 oz. can sliced black olives, drained
- 4 oz. mozzarella cheese, cubed
- ½ C. Parmesan cheese, shredded
- 1 C. bell pepper, diced
- ½ C. celery, diced
- ⅓ C. green onions, sliced
- 1¼ C. Italian dressing
- 1 tomato, diced

Cook pasta in boiling water as directed on package. Drain, rinse, and cool completely. Place pasta in a big bowl and add chopped pepperoni, black olives, mozzarella cheese, Parmesan cheese, bell pepper, celery, and green onions. Drizzle with Italian dressing. Gently fold in tomato. Chill at least 20 minutes before serving.

If you want to make this recipe before your trip, cook, drain, and cool the pasta; stir in green onions, celery, and ¼ cup of the dressing; then cover and chill overnight. Stir in all remaining ingredients before serving.

THAI GRILLED CAULIFLOWER
Makes 4 servings CAMPFIRE

INGREDIENTS
- 1 head cauliflower, cut in large florets
- Olive oil
- Salt and pepper to taste
- ¾ tsp. red pepper flakes
- ¾ tsp. garlic powder
- Sriracha hot sauce
- ⅛ C. mayonnaise
- ⅛ C. Thai sweet chili sauce

Brush skewers and cauliflower with oil. Mix salt and pepper, red pepper flakes, and garlic powder. Sprinkle over cauliflower. Arrange cauliflower on grill pan, cover with foil, and cook over medium heat until roasted and tender, about 8 to 10 minutes on each side.

Mix a few drops Sriracha with mayonnaise and chili sauce. Serve as dipping sauce with cauliflower.

CHAPTER 3: MAINS

ALFREDO BACON PIZZA
Makes 4 servings OVEN

INGREDIENTS
- 13.8 oz. tube refrigerated pizza crust dough
- 1 C. bacon-flavored or plain Alfredo sauce
- 1¼ C. mozzarella cheese, shredded and divided
- 10 oz. pkg. frozen chopped spinach, thawed, drained, and squeezed dry
- 2 or 3 plum tomatoes, thinly sliced
- 5 precooked bacon strips

Heat oven to 425°F. Coat a 12" pizza pan with cooking spray. Unroll the dough and press evenly into the prepped pan, making a small rim around outer edge. Spread the sauce over the dough and sprinkle with ½ cup of the cheese. Arrange the spinach and tomatoes over the cheese. Cut the bacon strips into 1" pieces and arrange over the top; sprinkle the remaining ¾ cup cheese over all. Bake for 15 minutes or until the crust is golden brown and the cheese is melted.

To make it oven-free, use flatbread instead of pizza dough, preheat your grill to medium-high heat, cover grates with greased foil, and grill the pizza until the cheese melts.

CHICKEN À LA RV

Makes 4 servings `STOVETOP`

INGREDIENTS

- 1 C. fresh mushroom, sliced
- ½ green bell pepper, minced
- ½ C. butter
- ½ C. flour
- 1 tsp. salt
- ¼ tsp. pepper
- 1½ tsp. chicken bouillon
- 1½ C. milk
- 1½ C. hot water
- 4 boneless, skinless chicken breast halves, cooked and chopped
- 4 refrigerator biscuits, baked as directed on package

In a medium skillet or pan over medium heat, sauté sliced mushrooms and minced green peppers in butter. Cook until vegetables are softened, about 5 minutes, and remove from heat. Stir in flour, salt, and pepper. Return to low heat and cook until mixture is bubbly, stirring constantly. Remove from heat and stir in chicken bouillon, milk, and water. Return to heat and bring to a boil for 1 minute, stirring constantly. Stir in chopped chicken, cooked until heated throughout.

To serve, set one split biscuit on each plate and spread additional butter over biscuits. Spoon a generous amount of the hot chicken mixture over biscuits on each plate.

MONTEREY MEATLOAF

Makes 4 to 6 servings `OVEN`

INGREDIENTS

- 1 lb. ground beef
- 1½ C. medium salsa
- ¼ C. Parmesan cheese, grated
- ¼ C. Monterey Jack cheese, shredded
- 1 egg
- 1 C. saltine crackers, crushed

Preheat oven to 350˚F. Grease a 5" x 9" loaf pan and set aside. In a large bowl, combine ground beef, salsa, grated Parmesan cheese, shredded Monterey Jack cheese, egg, and crushed saltine crackers. Mix by hand until well combined and shape mixture into a loaf. Place loaf in prepared pan and bake in oven for 1 hour or until internal temperature of meatloaf registers at 160˚F on a meat thermometer. Meatloaf is done when browned throughout and juices run clear.

CHILI ORANGE CHICKEN

Makes 4 servings SLOW COOKER

INGREDIENTS

- ¾ C. enchilada sauce
- ¼ C. BBQ sauce
- 1 tsp. salt, divided
- 1 T. chili powder
- 1 tsp. ground cumin
- 4 bone-in, skin-on chicken breast halves
- ⅓ C. orange marmalade
- ½ C. chopped cilantro
- 1 T. orange zest

In a large greased slow cooker, mix enchilada sauce, BBQ sauce, and ½ teaspoon of the salt. On a plate, mix chili powder, cumin, and remaining ½ teaspoon salt. Coat the chicken with the dry mixture and arrange in the cooker. Cover and cook on high for 2½ to 3 hours, until the internal temperature of the chicken reaches 165˚F.

Turn off the cooker; transfer the chicken to a serving plate. To the liquid in the cooker, stir in the marmalade, cilantro, and orange zest and serve over the chicken.

DELICIOUS CHILI

Makes 8 servings STOVETOP

INGREDIENTS

- 28 oz. can crushed tomatoes in juice
- 2 lbs. ground beef, cooked
- 1 small onion, chopped
- 2 cloves garlic, minced
- Two 15 oz. cans kidney beans
- 2 T. chili powder
- 1 T. distilled white vinegar
- Salt and pepper to taste

In a 2-quart saucepan over medium-high heat, place vegetable oil, cooked ground beef, chopped onions, and minced garlic. Cook until ground beef is heated and vegetables are softened. Drain pan of fat and stir in kidney beans, crushed tomatoes in juice, chili powder, and vinegar. Season with salt and pepper to taste. Bring chili to a boil, reduce heat, cover, and let simmer for 30 minutes.

SOUTHWEST CHICKEN BAKE

Makes 6 servings `CAMPFIRE`

INGREDIENTS

- 2 C. chopped chicken
- 1½ C. shredded Mexican cheese blend, divided
- 10.75 oz. can cream of mushroom soup
- 10.75 oz. can cream of celery soup
- 10 oz. can diced tomatoes with green chilis
- ¾ C. green onions, sliced
- 8 flour tortillas, cut into small pieces

In the oiled pot of a 10" Dutch oven, combine chicken, 1 cup cheese, both soups, tomatoes, and onions. Stir in tortilla pieces. Cover pot with lid and set on a ring of 11 hot coals; arrange 11 more coals on the lid. Cook 20 to 30 minutes or until hot and bubbly, rotating pot and lid several times. Remove lid, sprinkle with remaining ½ cup cheese, and let melt.

ONE-POT LASAGNA
Makes 6 servings STOVETOP

INGREDIENTS

- 1 T. vegetable oil
- 1 lb. ground turkey
- ½ tsp. garlic powder
- ½ tsp. onion powder
- ½ tsp. red pepper flakes
- Salt and black pepper to taste
- 6 oz. mini lasagna noodles (mafalda)
- 24 oz. jar marinara sauce
- 2 C. chicken stock
- ½ C. mozzarella cheese, shredded
- ¼ C. Parmesan cheese, grated
- ¾ C. cottage cheese

Heat the oil in a medium saucepan over medium-high heat. Add the ground turkey and cook until no longer pink, crumbling it while it cooks; drain and return to the saucepan.

Stir in the garlic powder, onion powder, pepper flakes, salt, and black pepper and cook for a minute or two. Stir in the noodles, marinara sauce, and stock. Bring to a boil, cover, and simmer for 20 minutes until the noodles are tender, stirring often.

Remove the pan from the heat and stir in half the mozzarella and Parmesan cheeses. Drop the cottage cheese in blobs over the top and sprinkle with the remaining mozzarella and Parmesan. Cover and let stand off the heat until melted. Stir gently before serving.

SUPER SLOPPY JOES
Makes 4 servings `STOVETOP`

INGREDIENTS
- 1 lb. ground beef
- 1 small onion, chopped
- 2 T. ketchup
- 1 C. stewed or fresh tomatoes, chopped
- 2 large green bell peppers, chopped
- 1 T. brown sugar
- 1½ tsp. apple cider vinegar
- 1½ tsp. Worcestershire sauce
- 1½ tsp. steak sauce
- ¼ tsp. garlic salt
- ⅛ tsp. ground mustard
- ⅛ tsp. paprika
- 4 hamburger buns

In a large saucepan, cook ground beef and onion. Cook thoroughly and stir in ketchup, tomatoes, bell peppers, brown sugar, apple cider vinegar, Worcestershire sauce, steak sauce, garlic salt, ground mustard, and paprika. Continue to cook, stirring frequently, until mixture is simmering and heated throughout. To serve, spoon mixture onto hamburger buns.

SANTA FE BURGERS
Make 4 servings `GRILL`

INGREDIENTS
- 1 lb. ground turkey
- 1 C. shredded Mexican cheese blend
- ¼ C. salsa
- ¼ C. tortilla chips, crushed
- ¼ C. green onion, chopped
- 1 tsp. smoked chili powder
- ½ tsp. garlic salt
- 4 Kaiser rolls

Grease the grill grate and preheat the grill on medium-high heat. In a bowl, combine ground turkey, Mexican cheese blend, salsa, tortilla chips, green onion, chili powder, and garlic salt; mix lightly, shape into four patties, and press an indentation in the top of each.

Grill until the internal temperature of the meat reaches 160°F, turning to brown both sides. During the last minute or two, spread butter on the cut sides of four Kaiser rolls and grill until lightly toasted. Serve burgers on toasted rolls with lettuce, tomato, red onion, and salsa.

TERIYAKI ONION BURGERS

Makes 6 servings `GRILL`

INGREDIENTS

- 1½ lbs. lean ground beef
- ½ C. teriyaki sauce, divided
- 3 oz. can French fried onions, crushed
- 6 hamburger buns, split
- 2 C. green cabbage, finely shredded

Grease the grill grate and preheat the grill on high heat. Mix the ground beef, ¼ cup plus 2 tablespoons of the teriyaki sauce, and the French fried onions; shape into six patties.

Grill the patties for 5 minutes on each side or until done to your liking, brushing occasionally with the remaining 2 tablespoons teriyaki sauce. Spritz cut sides of buns with cooking spray and grill until toasted. Serve burgers and cabbage on toasted buns.

HAWAIIAN PIZZA

Makes 4 to 6 servings `OVEN`

INGREDIENTS

- 14 oz. tube refrigerated pizza crust dough
- 1 C. pizza sauce
- Cooked Canadian bacon, chopped
- 8 oz. can pineapple chunks, drained
- 2 C. mozzarella cheese, shredded

Preheat oven to 350°F. Press refrigerated pizza crust dough evenly onto a lightly greased 10" to 12" pizza pan. Spread pizza sauce over pizza crust to within ½" from the edge. Sprinkle Canadian bacon over pizza sauce and spread pineapple chunks over Canadian bacon. Sprinkle shredded mozzarella cheese over pizza and bake in oven for 15 to 20 minutes or until crust is lightly browned and cheese is melted.

BROCCOLI & CARROT LASAGNA

Makes 6 servings OVEN

INGREDIENTS
- 2 C. broccoli, chopped
- 2 carrots, chopped
- 6 oz. mini lasagna noodles
- 10¾ oz. can cream of mushroom soup
- ¼ C. plus 2 T. Parmesan cheese, grated and divided
- ⅓ C. cottage cheese
- 1½ C. mozzarella cheese, shredded and divided
- ½ tsp. garlic powder
- ½ tsp. dried rosemary, crushed
- 1 tsp. paprika

Preheat oven to 375°F. In a small pot of water or vegetable steamer over medium heat, steam broccoli and carrots until tender. Fill a medium pot with water and bring to a boil over medium-high heat. Add lasagna noodles and cook until softened. In a separate bowl, combine cream of mushroom soup, ¼ cup Parmesan cheese, cottage cheese, and 1 cup shredded mozzarella cheese. Mix well and set aside ¾ cup of the mixture. To remaining mixture, add garlic powder, dried rosemary, and steamed broccoli and carrots. Mix well and set aside.

To assemble, in an 8" x 8" pan, layer half of the vegetable mixture and cover with half of the cooked lasagna noodles. Top noodles with remaining half of the vegetable mixture, followed by the remaining half of the noodles. Top with reserved ¾ cup cheese mixture. Sprinkle with remaining ½ cup shredded mozzarella cheese. Combine paprika and remaining 2 tablespoons Parmesan cheese and sprinkle over mozzarella. Cover pan with aluminum foil and bake for 30 minutes. Remove aluminum foil and bake for an additional 10 minutes.

MAINS

MEAT SAFETY GUIDELINES

The USDA recommends cooking dishes to the following minimum internal temperatures:

Fish: 145°F

Beef Roasts: 145°F (rare), 160°F (medium), 170°F (well-done)

Ground Beef: 160°F

Ground Poultry: 165°F

Chicken Breasts: 170°F

Whole Poultry and Parts (thighs, wings): 180°F

Pork (chops, tenderloins): 160°F

Ground Pork: 160°F

Egg Dishes: 160°F

Reheating Foods: 165°F or until hot and steaming

EASY SAUSAGE & CHICKEN STEW

Makes 8 servings `STOVETOP`

INGREDIENTS

- 3 T. olive oil
- 5 mild bratwurst or sausage links, casings removed
- 1 onion, chopped
- 1 shallot, chopped
- 3 carrots, chopped
- 1 chicken breast, cooked and diced
- 5 red potatoes, cut into chunks
- 15 oz. can cannellini beans, drained and rinsed
- 49 oz. can chicken broth
- ¼ C. Parmesan cheese, grated
- 1 tsp. dried thyme leaves
- Salt and black pepper to taste
- 5 C. fresh kale, chopped
- 3 T. flour
- ¾ C. cold water

In a big saucepan, heat the oil over medium heat. Slice the sausages and add them to the hot oil along with the onion and shallot and cook until the sausages are done, stirring occasionally. Add the carrots, chicken, potatoes, beans, broth, Parmesan, thyme, salt, and black pepper and simmer for 30 minutes, until everything is tender, stirring in the kale during the last 10 minutes.

In a small bowl, stir together the flour and water until smooth and stir into the stew until slightly thickened.

GARLIC SHRIMP TORTELLINI

Makes 8 servings `STOVETOP`

INGREDIENTS

- 19 oz. pkg. frozen cheese tortellini
- 1 head broccoli, cut into small florets
- ¼ C. olive oil
- 12 oz. shrimp, peeled and deveined, partially thawed if frozen
- 2 T. garlic, minced and divided
- ¼ C. butter
- ½ tsp. red pepper flakes
- ¼ C. flour
- 2 C. milk, plus more as needed
- 1 C. half-and-half
- 4 oz. cream cheese, cubed and softened
- ½ C. Parmesan cheese, shredded
- Salt and black pepper to taste

Cook the tortellini in a large saucepan according to package directions, adding the broccoli during the last 3 minutes of cooking time; drain and rinse with cool water and set aside.

Heat the now-empty pan over medium-high heat; add oil, shrimp, and 1 tablespoon of the garlic, cooking until shrimp turn pink, stirring occasionally. Transfer to a bowl and set aside.

Melt the butter in the empty pan over medium heat. Add the pepper flakes and the remaining 1 tablespoon garlic; cook about 30 seconds. Whisk in the flour until lightly browned. Gradually whisk in 2 cups milk and the half-and-half; cook for 6 to 8 minutes or until slightly thickened, whisking constantly. Stir in the cream cheese and Parmesan cheese, stirring until melted, adding a little more milk if the mixture is too thick. Season with salt and black pepper. Add the set-aside tortellini and broccoli and toss to combine. Top each serving with the set-aside shrimp.

BBQ PORK BURGERS

Makes 6 servings GRILL

INGREDIENTS
- 2 lbs. ground pork
- 1 tsp. ground ginger
- ½ C. green onions, chopped
- ¼ tsp. ground allspice
- Salt and black pepper to taste
- BBQ sauce
- 6 pineapple rings
- Butter
- 6 hamburger buns
- Spinach leaves
- 6 slices deli ham

Dump the ground pork, ginger, green onions, allspice, salt, and black pepper into a bowl and mix until just combined. Form six large patties and press an indentation into the top of each.

Grease the grill grates and preheat the grill on medium heat. Toss the patties on the grill and brush with BBQ sauce; cook with the lid closed until brown on the bottom, then flip and brush with more BBQ sauce. Cook until the internal temperature of the meat reaches 160°F; set aside for 5 minutes. In the meantime, toss the pineapple slices on the grate and heat until lightly browned, turning once. Butter the cut sides of the buns and grill until toasted.

To serve, put the spinach, burgers, more BBQ sauce, a slice of ham, and a grilled pineapple slice between the grilled buns.

SPINACH MANICOTTI

Makes 4 to 6 servings `OVEN`

INGREDIENTS

- 2 C. ricotta cheese
- 2 eggs
- 10 oz. pkg. frozen chopped spinach, thawed and drained
- 1 C. mozzarella cheese, shredded
- ½ C. Parmesan cheese, grated and divided
- 1½ T. sugar
- ⅛ tsp. salt
- ¼ tsp. pepper
- 10 to 12 large manicotti shells
- 48 or 60 oz. jar spaghetti sauce

In a medium bowl, combine ricotta cheese and eggs, mixing until blended. Stir in drained spinach, shredded mozzarella cheese, ¼ cup grated Parmesan cheese, sugar, salt, and pepper. Mix well and stuff mixture into the uncooked manicotti shells. Spread the spaghetti sauce evenly into the bottom of a 9" x 13" baking dish. Arrange stuffed manicotti shells in a single layer over sauce in pan. Pour remaining sauce over shells, cover dish tightly with aluminum foil, and chill in refrigerator for 8 hours.

Preheat oven to 400°F. Bake chilled manicotti in oven for 40 minutes. Sprinkle remaining ¼ cup grated Parmesan cheese over noodles and return to oven, uncovered, for an additional 15 minutes.

BLT SALAD

Makes 4 to 6 servings `NO-COOK`

INGREDIENTS

- 12 strips cooked bacon
- ¾ C. mayonnaise
- ¼ C. milk
- 1 tsp. garlic powder
- ⅛ tsp. pepper
- Salt to taste
- 1 head romaine lettuce, rinsed and torn
- 2 large tomatoes, chopped
- 2 C. seasoned croutons

Crumble bacon into small pieces. In a medium bowl, using a whisk, combine mayonnaise, milk, garlic powder, and pepper. Whisk thoroughly until blended and smooth. Season to taste with salt. In a large serving bowl, combine torn romaine lettuce, chopped tomatoes, and crumbled bacon. Toss until well incorporated. Pour dressing over salad and toss until evenly coated. Sprinkle croutons over salad and serve.

BACON-WRAPPED CHICKEN KEBABS

Makes 4 servings OVEN

INGREDIENTS

- ⅔ C. brown sugar
- 2 T. chili powder
- 1¼ lbs. boneless skinless chicken breasts
- 1 lb. bacon strips

Heat oven to 350°F. Line a rimmed baking sheet with foil and place a wire rack on top. Coat rack with cooking spray. Soak wooden skewers in water for 30 minutes or use side-by-side metal skewers.

Mix brown sugar and chili powder in a shallow bowl. Cut chicken into 1" cubes and cut bacon strips into thirds. Wrap one bacon piece around a chicken cube and coat in the brown sugar mixture; slide onto a skewer. Repeat with remaining bacon and chicken, putting four or five on each skewer.

Arrange skewers on prepared rack. Bake 30 to 35 minutes or until the chicken is done and the bacon is crisp.

To make it oven-free, preheat your grill to medium heat, cover grates with greased foil, and grill the meat skewers until the chicken is done and the bacon is crisp.

HAM & CHEESE CASSEROLE

Makes 4 to 6 servings OVEN

INGREDIENTS

- 8 eggs
- 1 C. milk
- Salt and pepper to taste
- 4 C. cooked ham
- 1 C. Cheddar cheese, shredded

Preheat oven to 350°F. In a large bowl, beat eggs until frothy. Add milk, salt, and pepper and mix well. Dice ham into small pieces. Stir diced ham and shredded Cheddar cheese into egg mixture. Pour mixture into a greased 9" x 13" baking dish and bake in oven for 40 to 50 minutes, until top of casserole is lightly browned.

MARINATED PORK TENDERLOIN
Makes 4 servings `GRILL`

INGREDIENTS
- ¼ C. soy sauce
- ¼ C. brown sugar
- 2 T. white cooking wine
- 1½ tsp. dried onion flakes
- 1 tsp. cinnamon
- 2 T. olive oil
- Pinch of garlic powder
- Two 1 lb. pork tenderloins

In a large zip-top bag, combine soy sauce, brown sugar, white cooking wine, dried onion flakes, cinnamon, olive oil, and garlic powder. Close bag and shake until well mixed. Place pork tenderloins in bag, seal, and place in refrigerator for 4 to 6 hours. Preheat grill to medium-high heat or place a large skillet over medium-high heat. Lightly oil the grate or skillet. Place marinated pork tenderloins on grill or in heated skillet. Discard the marinade. Grill or cook tenderloins for 15 to 20 minutes or to desired doneness, turning once. Slice tenderloins in half and serve.

BAJA BEEF TACOS
Makes 4 servings `STOVETOP`

INGREDIENTS
- 2 T. vegetable oil
- 1 onion, chopped
- 2 cloves garlic, minced
- 1 lb. ground beef
- 14½ oz. can diced tomatoes with jalapeños
- 4 oz. can diced green chilis, drained
- 1¼ oz. envelope taco seasoning
- Eight 8" flour tortillas
- Medium salsa

In a medium skillet over medium heat, heat vegetable oil. Sauté chopped onions and minced garlic in oil for 3 minutes. Add ground beef and cook, stirring occasionally, until browned throughout, about 6 minutes. Stir in diced tomatoes with jalapeños, drained green chilis, and taco seasoning. Bring mixture to a boil, reduce heat, and let simmer for 5 minutes.

To assemble tacos, place ½ cup of the meat mixture in the center of each flour tortilla. Top with some of the medium salsa, shredded lettuce, and shredded Cheddar cheese; fold in half. Place two tacos on each of four serving plates and serve.

BLUE CHEESE BURGERS

Makes 6 burgers   GRILL

INGREDIENTS

- 1½ lbs. ground beef
- ¼ C. blue cheese, crumbled
- 3 green onions, chopped
- ⅛ tsp. hot pepper sauce
- ½ tsp. Worcestershire sauce
- Salt and pepper to taste
- ½ tsp. dry mustard
- 6 hamburger buns

Preheat grill or place a large skillet over high heat. In a large bowl, combine ground beef, crumbled blue cheese, chopped green onion, hot pepper sauce, Worcestershire sauce, salt, pepper, and dry mustard. Mix by hand until well incorporated and shape mixture into six hamburger patties. Lightly oil the grate or spray skillet with non-stick cooking spray. Place burgers on hot grill or in hot skillet and cook for 5 minutes per side, until cooked to desired doneness. Serve on hamburger buns.

BLACK BEAN BURRITOS

Makes 4 burritos   STOVETOP

INGREDIENTS

- Four 10" flour tortillas
- ¼ C. vegetable oil
- 1 medium onion, chopped
- 1 red bell pepper, chopped
- 2 cloves garlic, minced
- 1 jalapeño pepper, seeded and minced
- Two 15 oz. cans black beans, drained and rinsed
- 8 oz. cream cheese, softened
- 1 tsp. salt
- ¼ C. fresh cilantro, chopped

Preheat oven to 350°F. Wrap tortillas in aluminum foil and place in heated oven for 15 minutes. In a 10" skillet over medium heat, place vegetable oil. Add chopped onion, chopped red bell pepper, minced garlic, and minced jalapeño pepper to skillet. Cook for 2 minutes until softened, stirring occasionally. Add rinsed beans to skillet and cook for an additional 3 minutes. Cut cream cheese into cubes and add to skillet. Cook for 2 minutes, until cream cheese is melted, and stir in salt and cilantro.

To assemble burritos, spoon a generous amount of the black bean mixture down the center of each warmed tortilla. Wrap tortillas to enclose filling and serve immediately.

LEMONADE CHICKEN

Makes 4 to 6 servings `CAMPFIRE`

INGREDIENTS
- 4½ lb. whole chicken
- Lemon pepper
- 12 oz. can lemon-lime soda
- Juice of 1 lemon

Rinse chicken and pat dry. Season inside and out with lemon pepper. Pour soda and lemon juice into the pot of a deep 12" Dutch oven; set chicken inside (breast side up) and cover with lid. Cook about 1½ hours on a ring of eight hot coals (with more coals on lid for browning) until meat tests done (minimum 165°F).

AMERICAN TUNA HOT DISH

Makes 4 to 6 servings `OVEN`

INGREDIENTS
- 2 lbs. russet potatoes, peeled and cubed
- 1 C. milk
- 1 C. mozzarella cheese, shredded
- ⅓ C. Parmesan cheese, grated and divided
- 2 eggs, beaten
- Three 6 oz. cans chunk light tuna, drained
- 4 green onions, chopped
- Salt and pepper to taste

Preheat oven to 400°F. In a large pot over high heat, place cubed potatoes and cover with water. Bring to a boil. Boil potatoes for 20 minutes, until tender. Drain pot and transfer all but 3 cups of the diced potatoes to a large bowl. Add milk, shredded mozzarella cheese, and 2 tablespoons Parmesan cheese. Using a hand mixer or potato masher, mash potatoes until almost smooth. Add beaten eggs and drained tuna to mashed potatoes and mix well. Fold in chopped green onions and season with salt and pepper to taste.

Transfer mixture to a lightly greased large casserole dish. Top with remaining grated Parmesan cheese. Bake in oven for 45 minutes or until tops of potatoes are golden brown.

SLOW & EASY PORK & SLAW COMBO

Makes 6 to 8 servings `SLOW COOKER`

INGREDIENTS

- 2 lbs. pork tenderloin
- 12 oz. can root beer
- 1¼ C. coleslaw dressing
- 14 oz. pkg. shredded coleslaw mix
- ½ green bell pepper, diced
- ½ red bell pepper, diced
- ½ C. onion, diced
- 3 T. parsley, chopped
- 18 oz. bottle BBQ sauce

Place pork tenderloin in a slow cooker; pour root beer over the top. Cover and cook on low for 8 hours, until pork shreds easily. Meanwhile, mix coleslaw dressing, coleslaw mix, bell peppers, onion, and parsley; chill until serving time.

Shred the cooked pork; discard the juices. Stir BBQ sauce into the shredded pork. Serve on buns topped with the slaw.

CAMP CASSEROLE

Makes 4 to 6 servings `STOVETOP`

INGREDIENTS

- 1 small head Napa cabbage, shredded
- 6 slices bacon, cooked and crumbled
- 3 C. cooked ham, diced
- 1 medium onion, sliced
- 1 T. butter
- 2 C. potatoes, cooked and diced
- ½ tsp. paprika
- Salt and pepper to taste

In a medium saucepan over medium heat, place shredded cabbage and ½ cup water. Cook for 5 minutes, until cabbage is tender. Drain cabbage and set aside. Crumble bacon into small pieces and chop cooked ham into small pieces. In a large skillet, place crumbled bacon and sliced onions, cooking until onions are softened. Add chopped ham, butter, cooked cabbage, and diced cooked potatoes. Mix well and season with paprika, salt, and pepper. Cook until mixture browns on the bottom, turn over in skillet, and cook until browned on other side.

CHICKEN QUESADILLAS

Makes 4 to 6 servings `STOVETOP`

INGREDIENTS

- 3 C. chicken, cooked and chopped
- 1¼ oz. envelope fajita seasoning
- 1 T. vegetable oil
- 2 green bell peppers, chopped
- 2 red bell peppers, chopped
- 1 onion, chopped
- Ten 10" flour tortillas
- 1 C. Cheddar cheese, shredded
- 1 C. Monterey Jack cheese, shredded

Preheat oven to 350'F. In a large saucepan over medium heat, combine chopped cooked chicken, fajita seasoning, chopped green bell pepper, chopped red bell peppers, and chopped onions. Cook for 10 minutes, stirring occasionally, until vegetables are tender. Divide chicken mixture evenly over half of each tortilla. Sprinkle each tortilla with some of the shredded Cheddar cheese and shredded Monterey Jack cheese. Fold each tortilla in half to enclose the filling. Place folded tortillas on a baking sheet and bake in oven for 10 minutes or until cheese has melted.

SEAFOOD QUICHE
Makes 6 to 8 servings OVEN

INGREDIENTS
- ¾ C. half-and-half
- 1 deep dish frozen piecrust
- 1 C. Swiss cheese, shredded
- 4 oz. can tiny shrimp, drained
- 6 oz. can crabmeat, drained
- 5 eggs
- 1 tsp. salt
- Pinch of sugar
- Pinch of nutmeg
- Pinch of cayenne pepper
- Pinch of pepper
- Three 3½ oz. pkgs. shiitake mushrooms

Preheat oven to 450°F. In a large skillet over medium-high heat, cook bacon until crisp. Remove bacon to paper towels to drain. If necessary, fit thawed piecrust into pie pan, crimping edges. Crumble bacon and sprinkle into unbaked piecrust. Sprinkle shredded Swiss cheese and shrimp over bacon. Shred crabmeat with a fork and arrange crabmeat over cheese and shrimp.

In a medium bowl, whisk together eggs, half-and-half, salt, sugar, nutmeg, cayenne pepper, and pepper; mix well. Carefully pour egg mixture over ingredients in piecrust. Clean and slice shiitake mushrooms. Arrange mushrooms over egg mixture in crust. Bake in oven for 10 minutes. Reduce oven temperature to 350°F and bake for an additional 25 to 30 minutes or until set and eggs are no longer runny. Remove quiche from oven and let stand for 10 minutes before slicing into wedges.

STEAK SALAD
Makes 4 servings GRILL

INGREDIENTS
- Grilled steak, sliced
- 1 large head lettuce, shredded or torn
- 3 small tomatoes, sliced
- 8 oz. sliced fresh mushrooms
- ¾ C. blue cheese, crumbled
- ¼ C. walnuts
- ⅓ C. vegetable oil
- 3 T. red wine vinegar
- 2 T. lemon juice
- ½ tsp. salt
- ⅛ tsp. pepper
- 1 T. Worcestershire sauce
- ⅛ tsp. liquid smoke flavoring

In a large bowl, combine shredded lettuce, sliced tomatoes, sliced mushrooms, crumbled blue cheese, walnuts, and sliced steak. In a small bowl, whisk together vegetable oil, red wine vinegar, lemon juice, salt, pepper, Worcestershire sauce, and liquid smoke flavoring. Mix until well combined and pour dressing over ingredients in bowl. Toss until evenly coated.

SWEET POTATO CHILI

Makes 4 servings (STOVETOP)

INGREDIENTS

- 2 T. olive oil
- 1 large onion, diced
- 2 sweet potatoes, peeled and diced
- 2 tsp. garlic, minced
- 2 T. chili powder
- 1 T. ground cumin
- ½ tsp. chipotle powder
- 2 tsp. salt
- 2⅔ C. water
- 15 oz. can black beans, drained and rinsed
- 15 oz. can crushed tomatoes
- 1 T. lime juice
- Optional toppings: sour cream, avocado, shredded cheese

Heat the oil in a big skillet over medium-high heat. Add the onion and sweet potatoes and sauté until slightly softened, stirring often. Add the garlic, chili powder, cumin, chipotle powder, and salt; heat for 30 seconds, stirring constantly. Add the water and bring to a simmer. Cover, reduce heat to maintain a gentle simmer, and cook for 10 minutes or until the sweet potatoes are tender. Stir in the black beans, tomatoes, and lime juice; heat to simmering, stirring often. Cook to slightly reduce the liquid.

Serve with desired toppings. Omit the cumin and chipotle powder for a less smoky flavor.

MEATBALL STEW PACKS

Makes 6 servings `CAMPFIRE`

INGREDIENTS

- 1 lb. each ground beef and Italian sausage
- 2 C. crumbled ciabatta bread
- 1/3 C. milk
- 1 egg
- 3 T. grated Parmesan cheese
- 1 small head cabbage, sliced
- 1 large onion, sliced and divided
- Garlic salt and black pepper to taste
- 15 oz. can tomato sauce
- 1 T. vegetable oil
- Butter

In a big bowl, combine meats, bread, milk, egg, and Parmesan cheese; mix well. Form into 24 meatballs. Divide all the cabbage and most of the onion among six 18" doubled squares of heavy-duty foil. Place four meatballs in each pack and season with garlic salt and pepper. Divide tomato sauce among the packs and seal foil well. Set all packs on medium-hot coals and cook 20 to 30 minutes or until meat is done, rotating packs several times.

BAKED CASHEW CHICKEN

Makes 4 to 6 servings `OVEN`

INGREDIENTS

- 2 C. uncooked white rice
- 1½ C. chicken broth
- 10¾ oz. can cream of chicken soup
- 10¾ oz. can cream of mushroom soup
- 2 T. soy sauce
- 3 C. chicken, cooked and chopped
- 1 C. cashews

Preheat oven to 375°F. In a medium pot, cook rice according to package directions until tender. In a large saucepan over medium heat, combine chicken broth, cream of chicken soup, cream of mushroom soup, and soy sauce. Bring mixture to a boil and stir in 2 cups of the cooked chopped chicken. Stir in remaining half of the cooked rice and cashews. Spread mixture evenly into a 9" x 13" baking dish. Bake in oven for 20 to 25 minutes, until heated throughout.

SHIITAKE MUSHROOM PASTA
Makes 4 to 6 servings   STOVETOP

INGREDIENTS
- 1 clove garlic, minced
- 1 small onion, chopped
- 1 T. olive oil
- 3 C. shiitake mushrooms, sliced
- ¼ C. white wine
- ¼ C. chicken broth
- ½ C. half-and-half
- Salt and pepper to taste
- 12 oz. pkg. angel hair pasta
- 2 T. Parmesan cheese, grated
- 2 tsp. dried parsley flakes

In a medium skillet over medium heat, sauté minced garlic and chopped onions in olive oil. Add mushrooms and mix well. Add wine and chicken broth, cooking until mixture reduces by half. Mix in half-and-half and season with salt and pepper to taste.

Meanwhile, in a large pot of lightly salted water, cook angel hair pasta according to package directions, for 6 to 8 minutes, until al dente. Drain pasta and place in large bowl. Pour mushroom mixture over pasta and toss until evenly coated. To serve, place pasta and sauce on plates and sprinkle some of the grated Parmesan cheese and some of the dried parsley flakes over each serving.

GARLIC POT ROAST
Makes 4 servings   OVEN

INGREDIENTS
- 4 lb. beef chuck roast
- ½ C. butter
- 1 T. onion salt
- 1 T. garlic salt
- ¼ C. sugar
- ¼ C. brown sugar
- Three ¾ oz. pkgs. brown gravy mix
- 4 large potatoes, peeled and diced
- 4 large carrots, peeled and diced
- ½ onion, sliced
- 2 C. water

Preheat oven to 325˚F. Lightly coat the beef chuck roast with butter. Sprinkle onion salt, garlic salt, sugar, brown sugar, and one package of brown gravy mix over roast. In a large roasting pan, evenly spread diced potatoes, diced carrots, and sliced onion. Sprinkle one package brown gravy mix over vegetables and place roast over potatoes and carrots. Sprinkle remaining brown gravy mix over roast and vegetables in pan. Add water and any remaining butter to pan. Cover roasting pan and bake in oven for 30 minutes. Reduce temperature to 300˚F and continue to bake for 2 hours and 15 minutes or until roast reaches desired doneness.

NEW ORLEANS CHICKEN

Makes 4 servings STOVETOP

INGREDIENTS

- 3 lb. whole chicken, skin removed
- ⅓ C. flour
- 1 T. vegetable oil
- ½ lb. smoked sausage
- 2 cloves garlic, minced
- 1 onion, chopped
- 2 red bell peppers, chopped
- 3 Roma tomatoes, chopped
- 1 tsp. brown sugar
- ¾ tsp. dried thyme
- ¾ tsp. dried oregano
- ½ tsp. salt
- ¼ tsp. allspice
- 1½ C. long grain white rice
- 2¼ C. chicken broth

Cut chicken into pieces and dredge in flour. In a large saucepan over medium heat, place vegetable oil. Brown chicken pieces for 8 minutes per side. Transfer browned chicken to a plate. Add smoked sausage, minced garlic, chopped onions, chopped red bell peppers, chopped tomatoes, brown sugar, thyme, oregano, salt, and allspice to pan. Cook for 10 minutes, stirring occasionally, until peppers are softened. Stir in rice and chicken broth. Place browned chicken pieces into rice mixture. Bring to a boil, reduce heat, and cover. Let cook for 25 minutes, until liquid is absorbed and juices run clear.

OVEN-FRIED CHICKEN

Makes 4 to 6 servings OVEN

INGREDIENTS

- ½ tsp. poultry seasoning
- 1 C. all-purpose baking mix (such as Bisquick)
- ⅓ C. chopped pecans
- 2 tsp. paprika
- ½ tsp. salt
- ½ tsp. dried sage
- ½ C. evaporated milk
- 3 or 4 lb. whole chicken, cut into 8 pieces
- Butter

Preheat oven to 350°F. Lightly grease a 9" x 13" baking dish and set aside. In a small microwave-safe bowl, place butter. Heat butter in microwave until melted and set aside. In a shallow dish, combine baking mix, chopped pecans, paprika, salt, poultry seasoning, and dried sage. Mix well. Place evaporated milk in a separate shallow dish. Dip chicken pieces in evaporated milk and roll in pecan mixture until fully coated. Place coated chicken pieces in prepared baking dish and drizzle with melted butter. Bake in oven for 1 hour or until juices run clear. Place fried chicken pieces on a serving plate and serve.

GLAZED FRANK KEBABS

Makes 6 servings   GRILL

INGREDIENTS
- 4 hot dogs
- 2 ears of sweet corn, shucked
- 1 red onion
- ½ red bell pepper
- ½ green bell pepper
- Cherry tomatoes
- ½ C. chili sauce
- 3 T. brown sugar
- 2 T. spicy brown mustard

Slice hot dogs and sweet corn into 1" pieces; slice red onion into wedges. Cut bell peppers into 1" pieces. Alternately thread pieces of hot dog, corn, onion, bell pepper, and a few cherry tomatoes on skewers and set aside.

Combine chili sauce, brown sugar, and spicy brown mustard in a bowl. Set kebabs on a grate over medium-low heat; brush skewers with some of the sauce mixture. Cover food with foil and grill about 5 minutes. Continue to cook slowly until veggies are tender, rotating kebabs every 5 minutes and brushing skewers with more sauce. Serve warm.

STUFFED PORTOBELLOS

Makes 4 servings GRILL

INGREDIENTS

- 4 large Portobello mushrooms
- 1 C. Italian dressing
- 16 oz. jar roasted red peppers, chopped
- 2 C. mozzarella cheese, shredded

Remove stems and gills from mushrooms and marinate with dressing in a zippered plastic bag for at least 1 hour. Drain and grill on stem side for 5 minutes. Flip over and fill caps with red peppers and cheese. Grill until cheese melts, 5 to 8 minutes more.

SOUTHERN FRIED CHICKEN SALAD

Makes 4 servings STOVETOP

INGREDIENTS

- 2 C. chicken, cooked and chopped
- 1 red bell pepper, chopped
- 1 green bell pepper, chopped
- 1 small red onion, chopped
- 1 small head romaine lettuce, rinsed and shredded
- 4 slices bacon
- 3 T. apple cider vinegar
- 1 T. honey
- ½ tsp. Dijon mustard
- ½ tsp. salt
- ¼ tsp. pepper

In a large bowl, combine chopped red bell pepper, chopped green bell pepper, chopped red onions, shredded lettuce, and cooked chicken pieces. In a medium skillet over medium-high heat, cook bacon until browned and remove bacon to paper towels to drain. Remove all but 2 tablespoons of the bacon drippings from the skillet. To bacon drippings, add apple cider vinegar, honey, Dijon mustard, salt, and pepper. Bring mixture to a low boil, stirring frequently, and pour over ingredients in bowl. Crumble drained bacon over salad and toss until well incorporated.

CHAPTER 4:
APPS, TREATS, AND EXTRAS

BACON CORN DIP

Makes 8 servings **STOVETOP**

INGREDIENTS

- 6 strips bacon, chopped
- 3 C. corn kernels, thawed if frozen; drained if canned
- ½ C. onion, diced
- ¼ C. red bell pepper, diced
- 1 jalapeño, seeded and diced
- 4 oz. cream cheese, cut into small cubes
- ¼ C. sour cream
- 2 green onions, thinly sliced
- 1 tsp. sugar
- ¼ tsp. salt
- ½ tsp. black pepper
- Crackers and/or tortilla chips for serving

Cook bacon until brown and crispy. Transfer to a paper towel-lined plate to drain; set aside until cool.

In a mixing bowl, combine the corn, onion, bell pepper, jalapeño, cream cheese, sour cream, green onions, sugar, salt, black pepper, and cooked bacon. Refrigerate for at least 1 hour before serving. Serve with crackers or tortilla chips.

WIDE-EYED COLD BREW

Makes 8 servings **NO-COOK**

INGREDIENTS
- ½ C. ground coffee
- Water
- Ice
- Half-and-half
- Sweetened condensed milk

The night before, put ground coffee into a 1-quart mason jar; fill the jar with water, cover, and let set overnight at room temperature.

The next morning, strain through cheesecloth into a clean mason jar; discard coffee grounds. Add water to the coffee to fill the jar.

To serve, fill a 1-pint jar with ice; fill ⅔ full with the coffee. Add a big splash of half-and-half and sweetened condensed milk to taste. Stir before serving.

BBQ BACON RANCH DIP

Makes 8 to 10 servings **NO-COOK**

INGREDIENTS
- 12 oz. cream cheese, softened
- ½ C. prepared ranch dressing
- ⅓ C. BBQ sauce
- ½ C. bacon bits
- ½ C. bell pepper (any color), diced
- 1 tomato, diced
- 1 C. Cheddar cheese, shredded
- Crackers or cut-up hamburger buns for serving

Mix cream cheese and ranch dressing in a bowl; spread mixture in a pie pan. Spread with BBQ sauce, bacon bits, bell pepper, tomato, and shredded Cheddar cheese. Chill at least 1 hour before serving with crackers or leftover hamburger buns (sliced, buttered, and toasted on the grill).

SKILLET OREO ROLLS

Makes 8 servings **OVEN**

INGREDIENTS

- 4 oz. softened cream cheese
- 1 T. sugar
- 6 crushed Oreo cookies
- 13 oz. tube refrigerated cinnamon rolls (8 ct.)

Heat oven to 375°F and grease a 10" cast iron skillet. In a bowl, stir together cream cheese, sugar, and Oreo cookies. Remove the rolls as a whole from tube of refrigerated rolls and unroll into a rectangle (make sure to buy the kind that can be unrolled); set aside the frosting packet. Spread the cream cheese mixture evenly over the rectangle; reroll, cut into individual rolls, and arrange in the prepped skillet. Bake for 15 to 20 minutes until done. Spread or drizzle the set-aside frosting over the top.

To make it oven-free, cook on low heat in a covered grill or cover the skillet and cook on a rack over a warm campfire, until the rolls are done and no longer doughy.

BACON FUDGE

Makes 64 bite-size pieces `STOVETOP`

INGREDIENTS
- 1 lb. diced bacon
- 16 oz. semisweet baking chocolate, chopped
- 14 oz. can sweetened condensed milk
- ¼ C. butter
- ¼ C. heavy cream
- 1 C. chopped toasted pecans

Line an 8" x 8" pan with foil; coat with cooking spray. Cook bacon; drain, cool, and crumble. In a saucepan, combine baking chocolate, sweetened condensed milk, butter, and heavy cream; cook over low heat, stirring until melted. Add toasted pecans and all but ¼ cup of the bacon to the chocolate; stir to combine. Spread into the prepped pan and sprinkle with the remaining bacon. Chill until firm before cutting into 1" squares.

SWEET TORTILLA ROLL-UPS

Makes 4 servings `CAMPFIRE`

INGREDIENTS
- 4 flour tortillas
- Butter, softened
- Cinnamon sugar

Spread tortillas with butter and sprinkle generously with cinnamon sugar. Roll up, spritz with cooking spray, and wrap in foil; set on a grate over medium coals until warm.

APPS, TREATS AND EXTRAS

BERRY ANGEL CAKES

Makes 4 servings   NO-COOK

INGREDIENTS
- 1 C. raspberries
- 1 C. strawberries
- 1 T. sugar
- 4 mini angel food cakes
- Whipped cream

Mash the strawberries and raspberries together with sugar. Let stand a few minutes until juicy. Divide berry mix among mini angel food cakes. If you're feeling fancy, top with some whipped cream.

LEMON-LEMON S'MORES

Makes 1 serving per 2 cookies   CAMPFIRE

INGREDIENTS
- Marshmallows
- Lemon curd
- Cookies and cream candy bars
- Lemon cookies

Toast marshmallow. Layer lemon curd, toasted marshmallow, and segments of cookies and cream candy bars between two lemon cookies.

PEACH & CHERRY CRISP

Makes 8 servings CAMPFIRE

INGREDIENTS

- 12 oz. bag frozen red tart cherries
- 4 fresh peaches, sliced, or 16 oz. bag frozen peaches
- ¼ C. sugar
- 2 T. water
- ⅔ C. old-fashioned oats
- ⅔ C. flour
- ½ C. brown sugar
- ⅓ C. butter, melted
- ½ tsp. cinnamon
- Vanilla yogurt

Thaw and combine frozen red tart cherries and fresh or frozen peaches in a doubled 9" x 9" foil pan. Stir in sugar and water. In a bowl, mix old-fashioned oats, flour, brown sugar, melted butter, and cinnamon; spread over fruit. Cover with greased foil and cook on a grate over medium heat 45 to 60 minutes. Move to warm embers and set coals on top of foil a few minutes to brown. Top with vanilla yogurt.

PARTY PASTRY S'MORES

Makes 1 serving per 1 toaster pastry   CAMPFIRE

INGREDIENTS
- Pink marshmallows
- Milk chocolate
  candy bars
- Rainbow sprinkles
- Toaster pastries

Toast pink marshmallow.
Layer segments of
milk chocolate candy
bars, toasted pink
marshmallow, and rainbow
sprinkles between a split
toaster pastry.

MINTY MIX S'MORES

Makes 1 serving per 1 graham cracker   CAMPFIRE

INGREDIENTS
- Marshmallows
- Mint chocolate candy
- Crushed peppermints
- Graham crackers

Toast marshmallow. Layer mint chocolate
candy, toasted marshmallow, and crushed
peppermints between spilt graham cracker.

CINNAMON SENSATION S'MORES

Makes 1 serving per 1 donut `CAMPFIRE`

INGREDIENTS

- Marshmallows
- Dark chocolate candy bars
- Cayenne pepper
- Cinnamon sugar cake donut

Toast marshmallow. Layer segments of dark chocolate candy bars, toasted marshmallow, and a sprinkle of cayenne pepper between split cinnamon sugar cake donut.

STRAWBERRY CREAM S'MORES
Makes 1 serving per 1 graham cracker CAMPFIRE

INGREDIENTS
- Marshmallows
- Cream cheese, softened
- Fresh strawberries, sliced
- Cinnamon graham crackers

Toast marshmallow. Layer toasted marshmallow, cream cheese, and strawberries between split cinnamon graham cracker.

S'MORE BURRITOS PLEASE!
Makes 1 serving CAMPFIRE

INGREDIENTS
- One 8" flour tortilla
- 2 to 3 T. crunchy peanut butter
- 3 T. miniature marshmallows
- 3 T. miniature chocolate chips

Cut one piece of foil about 12" long. Set tortilla on the center of the foil. Spread the peanut butter over the tortilla, almost to the edges. Sprinkle the marshmallows and chocolate chips over half of the peanut butter. Fold in the sides and then roll up the tortilla like a burrito, beginning with the chocolate chip side. Wrap foil around burrito in a flat pack. Place double-wrapped burrito on warm embers and cook for 5 to 15 minutes or until tortilla is warm and chocolate is melted. Move as needed to obtain even heating.

ZESTY ORANGE S'MORES

Makes 1 serving per 1 graham cracker   CAMPFIRE

INGREDIENTS

- Marshmallows
- Milk chocolate candy bars
- Orange zest
- Chocolate graham crackers

Toast marshmallow. Layer segments of milk chocolate candy bars, toasted marshmallow, and orange zest between split chocolate graham cracker.

BACON S'MORES

Makes 1 serving per 1 graham cracker CAMPFIRE

INGREDIENTS
- Marshmallows
- Crisp bacon
- Milk chocolate candy bars
- Graham crackers

Toast marshmallow. Layer toasted marshmallow, bacon, and segments of milk chocolate candy bars between split graham cracker.

CASHEW BROWNIE S'MORES

Makes 1 serving per 1 graham cracker CAMPFIRE

INGREDIENTS
- Marshmallows
- Brownie pieces
- Cashews, chopped
- Graham crackers

Toast marshmallow. Layer toasted marshmallow, brownie pieces, and cashews between split graham cracker.

LEMON COCONUT S'MORES

Makes 1 serving per 1 graham cracker **CAMPFIRE**

INGREDIENTS
- Marshmallows
- Lemon curd
- Toasted coconut
- Graham crackers

Toast marshmallow. Layer toasted marshmallow, lemon curd, and toasted coconut between split graham cracker.

APPLE PIE S'MORES

Makes 1 serving per 1 graham cracker **CAMPFIRE**

INGREDIENTS
- Marshmallows
- Granny Smith apple slices
- Cinnamon graham crackers

Toast marshmallow. Layer toasted marshmallow and apple slices between split cinnamon graham cracker.

JUDGING CAMPFIRE TEMPERATURES

Hold your hand about 4" over the coals and count the number of seconds you can hold your hand in place before it gets too hot to keep it there:

2 seconds = about 500°F (High heat)

3 seconds = about 400°F (Medium-High heat)

4 seconds = about 350°F (Medium heat)

5 seconds = about 300°F (Low heat)

CHOCO RASPBERRY S'MORES

Makes 1 serving per 1 graham cracker **CAMPFIRE**

INGREDIENTS
- Marshmallows
- Raspberry jam
- Dark chocolate candy bars
- Graham crackers

Toast marshmallow. Layer toasted marshmallow, segments of dark chocolate candy bars, and raspberry jam between split graham cracker.

CHOCOLATE BANANA S'MORES

Makes 1 serving per 1 graham cracker **CAMPFIRE**

INGREDIENTS
- Strawberry marshmallows
- Nutella or other hazelnut spread
- Banana slices
- Chocolate graham crackers

Toast strawberry marshmallow. Layer toasted strawberry marshmallow, Nutella, and banana slices between split chocolate graham cracker.

TROPICAL S'MORES
Makes 1 serving per 1 graham cracker   CAMPFIRE

INGREDIENTS
- Toasted coconut marshmallow
- White chocolate candy bars
- Fresh pineapple slices
- Graham crackers

Toast toasted coconut marshmallow. Layer marshmallow, segments of white chocolate candy bars, and fresh pineapple slice between split graham cracker.

SAILOR S'MORES
Makes 1 serving per 2 crackers   CAMPFIRE

INGREDIENTS
- Marshmallows
- Creamy peanut butter
- Milk chocolate bar
- Saltine crackers

Toast marshmallow. Spread peanut butter onto one side of each saltine cracker and place a segment of milk chocolate bar on one of the saltines. Place toasted marshmallow between two saltines.

INDEX

Note: Page numbers in **bold** indicate TOC lists of recipes by category.